# Success in Maths

**Rowena Onions**
**Chris Onions**
**Jacqueline Pendergast**
**Garry Pendergast**
Series Editor: Jayne de Courcy

Ages 9–11

**BOOK 4**

## Contents

Collins Educational
*An Imprint of HarperCollinsPublishers*

# The ⭐3 Steps to Success...

## Step 1 — Key skills practice

★ *Success in Maths Book 4* provides practice in a number of important Maths skills. These skills are the ones that your child needs to master in order to achieve a high level in the Maths National Test at the end of Key Stage 2. They build on the skills covered in *Success in Maths Books 1, 2* and *3*.

★ Each chapter takes one Maths skill and gives your child practice in it, using graded questions. Your child should write the answers, with working where necessary, on separate sheets of paper.

★ This in-depth practice ensures that your child achieves real understanding of each skill.

## Step 2 — Practice with National Test Questions

★ The book contains three sections of *National Test Questions*. These are past Test questions on the skills taught in the chapters.

★ Your child can do these Test questions immediately after working on the skills chapters. You might, however, prefer to wait and ask your child to do them a little later to check that the topics have been thoroughly mastered.

## Step 3 — Improving your child's performance

★ The book contains detailed *Answers and Guidance* to both the skills practice questions and the *National Test Questions*.

★ The authors, who are KS2 Test Examiners, provide detailed guidance, showing how to go about answering the questions in the best possible way.

★ In this way, you can work with your child to improve both skills and performance in the KS2 Maths National Test.

## Help with timing

★ As the Maths National Test papers are timed, it is important that your child learns to answer questions within a time limit.

★ Each skills chapter and each *Test Question* section gives target times for answering the questions. If you choose to, you can ask your child to time how long it takes to answer the questions. You can then compare your child's time against the target times provided. In this way, you will form a good idea of whether your child is working at the right rate to complete the Maths National Test papers successfully.

## Progression

★ *Success in Maths* is aimed at 9–11 year-olds who are in Years 5 and 6 of primary school. There is in-built progression: each book builds on skills covered in previous books.

★ To get the most out of *Success in Maths*, it is important that your child works through all four books in sequence. If you are buying this series for your child who is aged 9/10 (Year 5), then buy Books 1 and 2, and Books 3 and 4 at age 10/11 (Year 6). If your child is already in Year 6, then it is still advisable to work through from Book 1 to Book 4, to ensure that your child benefits from the progression built into the series.

## Note to teachers

★ This book, and the other five titles in the *Success in Maths* series, are designed for use at home and in schools in Years 5 and 6. They focus on the key Maths skills that will raise children's performance in the Maths National Test.

★ You can use the books in class or give them to children for homework to ensure that they are fully prepared for their Maths National Test.

**What's it all about?**

★ This chapter reminds you how to estimate fractions of shapes, and how to express these fractions as percentages.

★ It also reminds you how to apply this knowledge to pie charts. **Write your answers on a separate sheet of paper, showing your working.**

> To estimate a fraction of a shape, you need to divide up the whole shape, either in your head or on paper.

> Remember that $\frac{4}{4} = 1$, $\frac{8}{8} = 1$, and so on.

**1** Divide up these shapes and then estimate what fraction of the shape is shaded. The first one is done for you.

a) 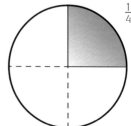  $\frac{1}{4}$ is shaded

c)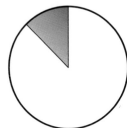

b)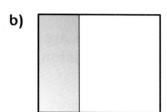

d)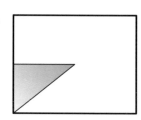

> Divide up the shapes very carefully. All the sections **must** be equal in size.

**2** Sometimes it is a little more difficult and you have to divide up the shaded part of the shape as well. Divide up these shapes and then estimate what fraction of the shape is shaded. The first one is done for you.

a) 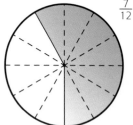  $\frac{7}{12}$ is shaded

c)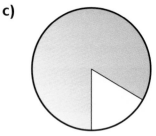

b)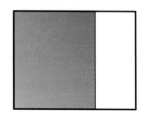

d)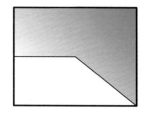

> Remember, the whole shape is 100%.

**3** Look again at the shapes in questions 1 and 2. Write what percentage of each shape is shaded. Give your answers to 1 decimal place (dp) where necessary.

**4** Each of these pie charts shows the sales on a fruit stall. The red section shows the sales of apples. The total amount of fruit sold is shown beneath each pie chart. Where necessary, give your answers to the nearest kilogram.

Estimate the weight of apples sold on each stall. The first is done for you.

**a)** 200 kg

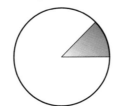

Approximately $\frac{1}{8}$ of the sales are of apples.

$\frac{1}{8} \times 200 = 25$

Approximately 25 kg of apples are sold.

**b)** 400 kg      **c)** 1000 kg      **d)** 500 kg

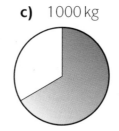

**5** These pie charts show the sales of three rival fruit shops. Which shop sells the greatest weight of bananas? Explain how you know.

Shop A      Shop B      Shop C

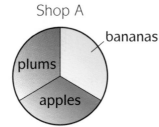
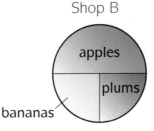

Total sales: 600 kg      Total sales: 900 kg      Total sales: 800 kg

## Test question

Some children work out how much money a shopkeeper gets from selling fruit. They use a pie chart to show this.

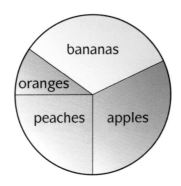

**Mrs Binns**

Mrs Binns gets a total of £1000.

Estimate how much Mrs Binns gets for selling **peaches**.

Answers and Guidance are given on p.36.      *How long did you take?*

# 2 Using your calculator

**What's it all about?**

★ This chapter gives you practice in using your calculator and interpreting the display accurately.

★ You are allowed to use a calculator in Paper B of your Maths National Test. It is important that you do use it when you are allowed to.

> Using your calculator correctly will help you save time and can improve the accuracy of your work.

Your calculator probably looks like this.

If you have a more complex calculator, identify the keys which do the same thing as those shown here and use them for the work in this chapter.

Some calculators have a ✱ symbol for multiplication and a ／ for division.

When you use your calculator to find answers, you must have an estimate of the answer in your head.

**1** Use your calculator to answer these questions. The order in which you should press the keys has been written for the first question of each different type.

> **Remember:** Always clear the calculator by pressing **AC** before starting work on a calculation.

**a)** 320 × 15     Press: `AC` `3` `2` `0` `×` `I` `5` `=`
Display shows: 4800

**b)** 42.8 × 18   **c)** 301 × 1.5   **d)** 1.66 × 52   **e)** 48.6 × 27.4

**f)** 114.5 ÷ 0.25   Press: `AC` `I` `I` `4` `.` `5` `÷` `0` `.` `2` `5` `=`
Display shows: 458

**g)** 108 ÷ 9.6                    **i)** 47 684 ÷ 18.2

**h)** 124.3 ÷ 1.25               **j)** 230.275 ÷ 15.1

**2** If the question you are doing is about money, you must be very careful to make sure you have two figures after the decimal point. You may need to add a zero to the calculator display. Try these. The first one is done for you.

**a)** £16.55 × 4     Press: `AC` `I` `6` `.` `5` `5` `×` `4` `=`
Display shows: 66.2
**Answer:** £66.20

**b)** £48.20 ÷ 4   **c)** £156 ÷ 8   **d)** £147 ÷ 16   **e)** £64.15 × 8

**3** In these questions there is a mixture of £ and pence. Be careful! The first one is done for you.

**a)** £6.68 + 65p     Press: `AC` `6` `.` `6` `8` `+` `0` `.` `6` `5` `=`
Display shows: 7.33
**Answer:** £7.33

**b)** £4.59 + 75p   **c)** £8.57 + 97p   **d)** £7.28 − 78p   **e)** £14.65 − 85p

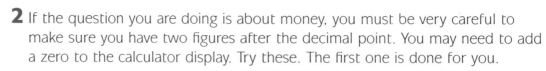

Some fractions, such as $\frac{1}{6}$, have no exact decimal equivalent. For $\frac{1}{6}$, the calculator display shows 0.1666666666666. It is normal to round this fraction to 2 or 3 decimal places, as 0.17 or 0.167.

**4** Work out the equivalent decimal form of these fractions.

**a)** $\frac{3}{8}$   Press:    Display shows: 0.375

**b)** $\frac{1}{2}$   **c)** $\frac{3}{4}$   **d)** $\frac{1}{5}$   **e)** $\frac{2}{5}$   **f)** $\frac{1}{8}$   **g)** $\frac{1}{3}$   **h)** $\frac{4}{5}$   **i)** $\frac{5}{8}$

Now put the fractions in order of size starting from the smallest.

**5** Find as many fractions as you can that have no exact decimal equivalent (like $\frac{1}{6}$).

**6** When questions have brackets, or more than one part, you can use the memory key on your calculator. Try these. The first one has been done for you.

**a)** $(24 + 15) \times (18 + 23)$   Press: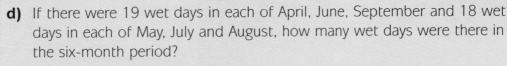

Display shows: 1599

If you want to clear the memory on this type of calculator, press the M- key.

**b)** $(26 + 24) \times (16 + 14)$      **d)** $(34 + 10) \div (28 - 6)$

**c)** $(35 - 18) \times (53 - 35)$      **e)** $(39 + 5) \div (26 - 18)$

**7** Use your calculator to answer these questions.

**a)** 1738 people went to a show. Each paid £1.75. How much money was collected?

**b)** Write the missing number. $622.3 \div \boxed{?} = 24.5$

**c)** Complete this number sentence. $356.2 \times \boxed{?} = 5414.24$

**d)** If there were 19 wet days in each of April, June, September and 18 wet days in each of May, July and August, how many wet days were there in the six-month period?

**e)** During June at a zoo there were 16 days when 317 people visited and 14 days when 326 people visited. How many people went to the zoo that month?

Don't forget to estimate the answer first.

## Test question

2753 people go to a sports event.

Each person pays £2.30 for a ticket.

What is the **total** amount of **ticket money** collected?

£ _____

Programmes cost **65p** each.

The total money from programme sales is **£612.95**.

How many programmes are sold?

Show your method. You may get a mark.

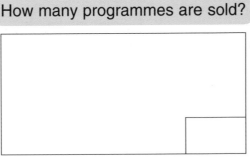

# 3 Area and perimeter

**When you split the shapes, remember to mark on all the necessary measurements – you may need them.**

**There is more than one way of splitting each shape.**

**1** Copy these compound shapes and split them into rectangles. The first one has been done for you.

**a)**

can split into

**b)**

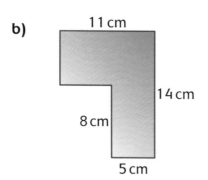

11 cm
14 cm
8 cm
5 cm

**d)**

10 cm
9 cm
6 cm
15 cm

**c)**

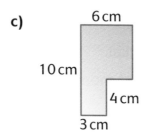

6 cm
10 cm
4 cm
3 cm

**e)**

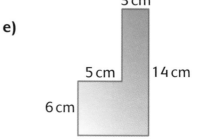

3 cm
5 cm
14 cm
6 cm

**Whichever way you split the shape, you should end up with the same total area. Try different ways until you are sure you understand this.**

**2** Now calculate the areas of each part of the compound shapes in question 1. The first one has been done for you.

**a)**

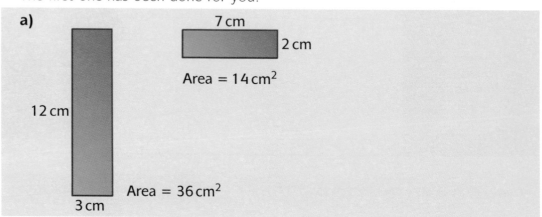

7 cm
2 cm
Area = 14 cm²

12 cm
Area = 36 cm²
3 cm

**The area of a rectangle is base × height. Look back at Book 2, Chapter 5 and Book 3, Chapter 8, if you need to.**

**3** Now calculate the total area of the same shapes. The first has been done for you.

**a)** Total area = 36 cm² + 14 cm² = 50 cm²

Add the areas of both parts together to find the total area.

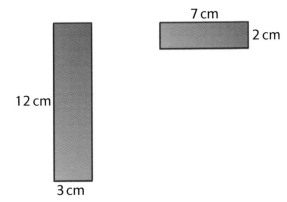

**4** Finally, calculate the perimeters of the shapes in question 1. The first has been done for you.

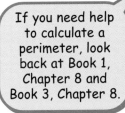

If you need help to calculate a perimeter, look back at Book 1, Chapter 8 and Book 3, Chapter 8.

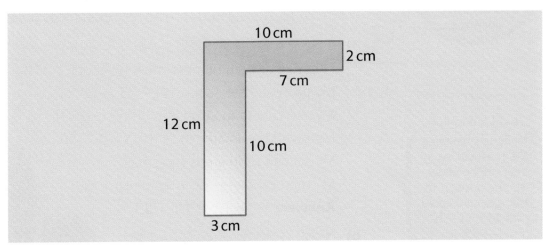

**a)** Perimeter = 10 + 2 + 7 + 10 + 3 + 12 = 44 cm

## Test question

Calculate the total area and the perimeter of this shape.

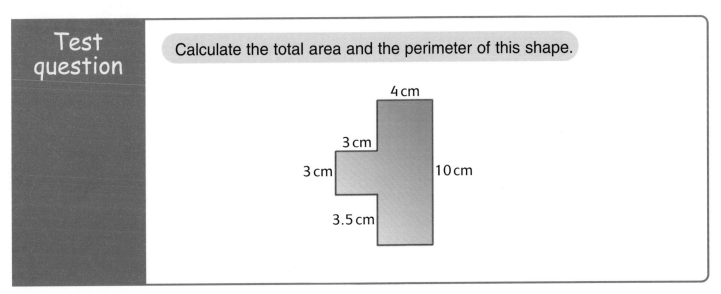

Answers and Guidance are given on pp.37–38.

 **How long did you take?**

**What's it all about?**

★ This chapter shows you how to solve maths problems by making the best use of your knowledge of numbers and of the information you are given.

★ It also reminds you how to estimate and how to use trial and improvement methods.

> Consecutive means 'one after another', for example, 67, 68 and 69 are consecutive numbers.

**1** In many mathematics problems, a good way to start is by making an 'educated guess', or **estimate**. Then you need to try out your estimate and change it if necessary. This is called the **trial and improvement** method.

Find three consecutive numbers that add up to give the answer shown. Write down all the steps you take. The first example is done for you.

**a)** 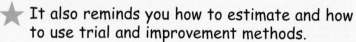 + + = 39

I know that each number must be about $\frac{1}{3}$ of the answer so:

My first estimate: 13 + 14 + 15 = 42

My estimate is too big.

My second estimate: 11 + 12 + 13 = 36

My second estimate is too small.

My third estimate: 12 + 13 + 14 = 39

**Answer:** 12 + 13 + 14 = 39

> Numbers can also be consecutive in descending order, so the answer to the example could be 14 + 13 + 12 = 39.

**b)** + + = 138

**c)** + + = 102

**d)** + + = 225

**2** Use your knowledge of numbers to help you complete the following sums. The first one is done for you.

**a)** × = 351

Using my knowledge of tables, I know that the single-digit number cannot be even and cannot be 5 or 1.

Using my knowledge that division is the inverse of multiplication, I try:

351 ÷ 3 = 117   too many digits

351 ÷ 7 = 50.1428…   not a whole number

351 ÷ 9 = 39

**Answer:** 39 × 9 = 351

> Look back at Book 1, Chapter 5 and Book 3, Chapter 7.

**b)** × = 504

**c)** × = 448

**d)** × = 768

**e)** × = 348

**f)** × = 539

**3** Each of these numbers is the result of multiplying a smaller number **by itself**. Find the smaller numbers. The first one has been done for you, and the second one has been started.

**a)** 729 ◆ × ◆ = 729

I use my knowledge of tables.

I know the answer must be more than 12 (as $12 \times 12 = 144$) and less than 30 (as $30 \times 30 = 900$), and an odd number.

First estimate: 29

$29 \times 29 = 841$

My estimate is too big.

Second estimate: 27

$27 \times 27 = 729$

**Answer:** $27 \times 27 = 729$

**b)** 324 ◆ × ◆ = 324

First estimate: ◆

My estimate is too big/too small.

Second estimate: ◆

My second estimate is too big/too small

and so on…

Now use the **same** number three times in each sum.

**c)** ◆ × ◆ × ◆ = 343

**d)** ◆ × ◆ × ◆ = 2197

**e)** ◆ × ◆ × ◆ = 1728

**f)** ◆ × ◆ × ◆ = 4913

**4**

Use each of the cards once only in each question.

Lay them out in a vertical addition (as shown), to complete the addition sum with an answer which is:

**a)** more than 1200 and less than 1300

**b)** more than 800 and less than 900

**c)** between 700 and 800.

### Test question

Write the same two-digit number three times to complete this.

$( \boxed{\phantom{00}} \times \boxed{\phantom{00}} ) - \boxed{\phantom{00}} = 506$

Answers and Guidance are given on p.38.

**How long did you take?**

🕐 *You should be able to complete these questions in 10 minutes*

**1** The outer ring of this spinner has **8 sections** labelled with the numbers **1 to 5**.

The inner ring has **12 equal sections** on it.

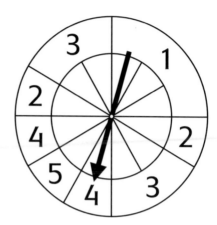

Laura spins the pointer.

✏️ Which number is the pointer most likely to stop on?

1 mark

✏️ Give a reason for your answer.

1 mark

What is the probability of getting an even number on this spinner?

✏️ Give your answer as a fraction.

1 mark

**2** Nicola has **£50**.

She buys **3 flowerpots and a spade**.

How much money does she have left?

Show your **method**. You may get a mark.

✏️ £

Spades
£9.65
each

Rakes
£7.75
each

Large flower pots
£12.95
each

2 marks

Seeds are **£1.45** for a packet.

Steffan has **£10 to spend on seeds**.

What is the greatest number of packets he can buy?

✏️

£1.45
seeds

1 mark

**3** Lindy has **4 triangles**, all the same size.

She uses them to make a star.

Not to scale.

Show your **method**. You may get a mark.

Calculate the perimeter of the star.

|  |
|---|
| cm |

*2 marks*

**4** Write the three missing digits.

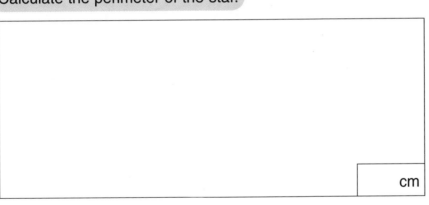

$$\boxed{\phantom{0}}\boxed{\phantom{0}} \times \boxed{\phantom{0}} = 371$$

*1 mark*

# 5 Division

**What's it all about?**

★ This chapter gives you practice in division, with and without a calculator.

★ In your Maths National Test you may be asked to solve problems using your knowledge of division, or to work out a division sum.

> It is important to have a rough idea of the answer you are expecting when you do a long division sum.

**1** Give an approximate answer for each of these divisions. Round the numbers to the nearest 100 or 10 as appropriate. The first one has been done for you.

a) $472 \div 52$    $450 \div 50 = 9$

b) $718 \div 23$    d) $622 \div 34$    f) $597 \div 44$    h) $892 \div 14$

c) $392 \div 42$    e) $882 \div 58$    g) $992 \div 17$

**2** Use a calculator to find the answers to the division sums in question 1. Round your answers to 2 dp if necessary.

Were your estimates in question 1 reasonably accurate?

**3** Solve these by long division. Do not use a calculator!

The first one has been done and explained for you.

> Look closely at the explanation written by the side. You really need to understand what you are doing if your work is going to be accurate.

a)
```
      21
28)588
      56
      28
      28
       0
```
The problem is divide 588 by 28. First try to divide the hundreds. You cannot divide 5 hundreds into 28 parts, so you need to change them into tens.

You have 58 tens. 58 tens divided by 28 is 2 tens. Write this in the tens column of the answer. This uses 56 tens and leaves you with 2 tens and 8 units = 28 units.

Divide these units by 28,    $28 \div 28 = 1$ unit.
Write this in the units column.

b) 37)851    d) 24)768    f) 18)972    h) 45)990

c) 14)504    e) 27)918    g) 41)943

**4** Now solve these by long division. Do not use a calculator! All these examples have a remainder. The first one has been done for you.

**a)**

$$\begin{array}{r} 29 \quad \text{r } 16 \\ 29\overline{)857} \\ \underline{58} \\ 277 \\ \underline{261} \\ 16 \end{array}$$

First try to divide the hundreds. You cannot divide 8 hundreds into 29 parts, so you need to change them into tens. You have 85 tens. 85 tens divided by 29 is 2 tens. Write this in the tens column. This uses 58 tens and leaves you with 27 tens and 7 units = 277 units.

Divide these units by 29, 277 ÷ 29 = 9 units. This uses 261 units and leaves a remainder of 16. Write the 9 in the units column. Write that you have a remainder of 16.

**b)** $23\overline{)632}$　　**d)** $35\overline{)388}$　　**f)** $34\overline{)489}$

**c)** $21\overline{)648}$　　**e)** $18\overline{)579}$　　**g)** $24\overline{)754}$

**5** Redo question 4, using a calculator. Round your answers to 2 dp.

**6** You can also write the remainder as a fraction. For instance in 4(a) above the answer is 29 r 16. Written as a fraction, it would be $29\frac{16}{29}$.

Now try these. This time write your remainder as a fraction.

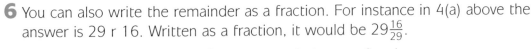

**a)** $24\overline{)628}$　　**c)** $28\overline{)589}$　　**e)** $32\overline{)872}$

**b)** $37\overline{)796}$　　**d)** $19\overline{)487}$　　**f)** $23\overline{)854}$

**7** When you are asked to divide numbers, it is easier to use a calculator if you are allowed to. Try these, rounding your answers to 2 dp.

**a)** $10\,764 \div 129$

**b)** $23\,682 \div 284$

**c)** $69\,382 \div 962$

**d)** $4639 \div 132$

**e)** $78\,062 \div 529$

**f)** $6898 \div 462$

**Test question**

Answer this question. Do not use a calculator.

$572 \div 16 =$

Answers and Guidance are given on pp.39–40.

 **How long did you take?**

# 6 Volume

**What's it all about?**

★ In this chapter you will find the volume of objects by counting centimetre cubes.

★ You will revise how to calculate the volume of cubes and cuboids.

> **Volume** is the amount of space a solid takes up.
>
> For a shape made up of four centimetre cubes, we say the volume is 'four cubic centimetres' and we write it as $4\,cm^3$.

**1** These shapes are made up of centimetre cubes. Each shape is one layer deep. What is the volume of each shape? The first one is done for you.

**a)**

There are 25 cubes in the shape. The volume is $25\,cm^3$.

**b)**

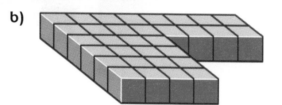

**d)**

**c)**

**e)**

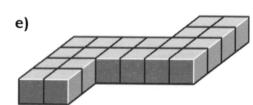

**2** When you calculate the volume of a shape which is more than one layer deep, you need to calculate the volume of one layer and then multiply by the number of layers.

Find the volume of each shape. The first one is done for you.

**a)**

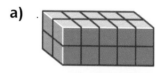

There are 2 layers. There are 10 cubes in each layer. The volume is $20\,cm^3$.

> For calculating (rather than counting) the volume of more complicated shapes, it is often easier to split the shape up into two (or more) cuboids, calculate the volume of each one and add them together.

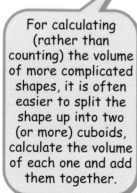

**b)**

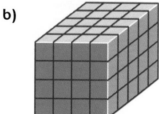

**d)**

**c)**

**e)**

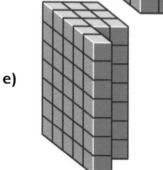

**3** To calculate the volume of a cube or a cuboid, you multiply the base width by the base length by the height. Calculate the volume of each of these shapes.

a)
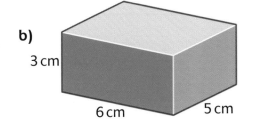

c)
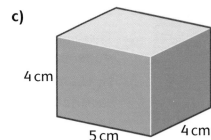

b)

d)
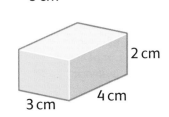

**4** Solve these problems about volume.

a) A cuboid has a volume of $16\,cm^3$. Its height is 2 cm and its base length is 4 cm. What is its base width?

b) A cuboid has a volume of $8\,cm^3$. Make rough sketches of three possible shapes for this cuboid. Label the base length, the base width and the height for each shape.

## Test question

This cuboid is made from centimetre cubes.

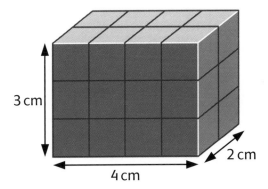

It is 4 centimetres by 3 centimetres by 2 centimetres.

What is the **volume** of the cuboid?

☐ cm³

Another cuboid is made from centimetre cubes.

It has a volume of **30 cubic centimetres**.

What could the **length**, **height** and **width** be?

length ☐ cm     height ☐ cm     width ☐ cm

Answers and Guidance are given on p.40.
 **How long did you take?**

**What's it all about?**

★ This chapter reminds you how to calculate the mean, mode and median of a set of numbers or data.

★ In the Maths National Test you may have to answer questions about the mean, mode and median, as well as calculate them.

> The **mean** of a set of numbers is often called the **average** of the numbers. The set of numbers is often called a set of **data**.

**1** You find the mean of a group of numbers by adding the numbers together and then dividing the total by the number of numbers.

Calculate the mean of each of these groups of numbers. The first one is done for you.

> Use a calculator for the bigger numbers if you want to.

**a)** 3, 6, 2, 4, 5
**Working:**
Total of all the numbers = 3 + 6 + 2 + 4 + 5 = 20
Number of numbers = 5
Mean = 20 ÷ 5 = 4
**Answer:**
The mean of the numbers is 4.

> The mean cannot be higher than the highest number nor lower than the lowest number in the set of data.

**b)** 3, 8, 9, 4, 6, 7, 5          **d)** 58, 39, 47, 60, 32, 40

**c)** 5, 9, 9, 8, 6, 7, 5, 8, 6      **e)** 114, 138, 120, 131, 111, 128, 126

**2** Try these problems.

**a)** During May a cricketer scores 25, 52, 0, 38, 2, 78, 102 and 7 runs. What is his mean score for the month?

**b)** A workman earns the following wages each day. Monday £60, Tuesday £74, Wednesday £83, Thursday £64, Friday £59. What is his average (mean) daily wage?

**c)** The class mean for the collection of computer vouchers was 14 vouchers. If there are 30 children in a class, how many vouchers did they collect?

**d)** The mean rainfall for three days was 12 mm. If it rained 6 mm on the first day and 14 mm on the second day, what was the rainfall on the third day?

**3** The **mode** of a set of numbers is the most commonly occurring number in the set. Find the mode(s) of these sets. The first one is done for you.

> If two values (numbers) occur the same number of times and they both appear more than any other value, the set of data has **two modes** and is **bi-modal**.

**a)** 18, 14, 10, 16, 15, 14, 11, 15, 14, 20, 18, 14, 11, 20, 14

The mode is 14 since 14 occurs five times, and the others only once or twice.

**b)** 28, 76, 64, 23, 28, 28, 90, 23, 23, 27, 28, 23, 23, 34

**c)** 56, 42, 33, 56, 21, 33, 56, 55, 50, 56, 34, 98, 96, 34, 21, 54, 34, 31

**d)** 11, 12, 11, 13, 11, 12, 13, 11, 11, 13, 12, 13, 13, 12

**4** Solve these problems.

**a)** A group of children sit a spelling test. The results are as follows.

14, 6, 12, 10, 10, 12, 14, 12, 9, 12, 15, 8, 19, 20, 12

What is the modal score?

**b)** A class of children record their shoe sizes as follows.

2, 2, 2, 3, 5, 3, 5, 1, 13, 12, 2, 4, 2, 2, 3, 5, 1, 2, 2, 3, 4, 5, 1, 1, 3

What is the modal shoe size?

**c)** Ten newspapers are on sale in a shop. If they cost 25p, 30p, 50p, 35p, 30p, 45p, 30p, 25p, 35p, 40p, what is the modal price?

**d)** Write five different sets of numbers. Each set should have a mode of 17.

The word **mode** is a noun. The adjective made from the noun is **modal**, so we talk about a 'modal score' or a 'modal size'.

**5** The **median** is the middle value in a set of data.

Find the median of each of these sets of numbers. The first one is done for you.

**a)** 25, 27, 25, 18, 45, 43, 28, 26, 37, 38, 18

Put in order, the data look like this.
18, 18, 25, 25, 26, 27, 28, 37, 38, 43, 45

The median is 27.

**b)** A basketball player scores the following numbers of points in a sequence of games: 28, 40, 21, 35, 20, 42, 41. What is his median score?

**c)** A workman earns the following wages each day: Monday £60, Tuesday £74, Wednesday £83, Thursday £64, Friday £59. What is his median daily wage?

**d)** Eleven newspapers are on sale in a shop. If they cost 25p, 30p, 50p, 40p, 30p, 40p, 45p, 30p, 25p, 35p, 40p, what is the median price?

It is best to rewrite the scores so that they are in order. This makes it much easier to find the middle score.

In a set of data with an even number of values, you will have two medians.

**6** Find the mean, mode and median of each of these sets of data.

**a)** 28, 27, 18, 35, 42, 19, 26, 32, 19, 26, 31, 26, 35

**b)** 25p, 40p, 35p, 40p, 30p, 30p, 45p, 50p, 25p, 30p, 35p

**c)** £25, £38, £38, £28, £36, £31, £35

**d)** 10.6, 11.2, 10.7, 11.2, 10.8, 10.7, 11.1

### Test question

Christine records the figures for her long jump practices.
The figures are in metres.

| 3.4 | 3.7 | 3.6 | 3.9 | 3.1 | 3.6 | 3.4 | 3.4 | 3.8 |
| 3.9 | 3.2 | 3.4 | 3.8 | 3.1 | 3.7 | 3.4 | 3.2 | 3.4 |

Find the mean, modal and median length of jump.

Answers and Guidance are given on p.41.

 **How long did you take?**

# 8 Rotational symmetry

**What's it all about?**

★ This chapter reminds you about rotational symmetry.

★ You will practise rotating shapes about a given point.

Rotations are clockwise unless you are told otherwise.

You can use tracing paper to help.

**1** Rotate each of these shapes around the point shown on the graph. The first one has been done for you.

**a)** Rotate shape A through 180°.

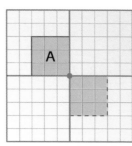

**b)** Rotate shape B through 90° clockwise.

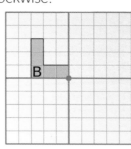

**c)** Rotate shape C through 270° clockwise.

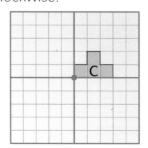

**d)** Rotate shape D through 90° clockwise.

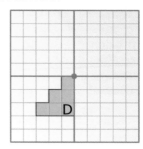

**2** Now try these. Use tracing paper to help you.

**a)** Rotate shape E through 180°.

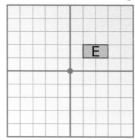

**b)** Rotate shape F through 270°.

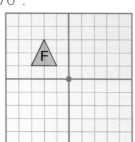

**c)** Rotate shape G through 90°.

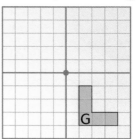

**d)** Rotate shape H through 270°.

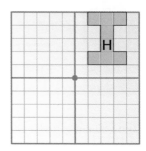

Notice that these shapes do not touch the point of rotation. Try using tracing paper first, to see what happens when you rotate them.

**3** Now try rotating these shapes.
The first one has been done for you.

**a)** Rotate the shape through
180° about point A.

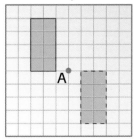

**b)** Rotate the shape through
90° about point B.

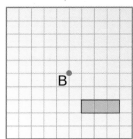

**c)** Rotate the shape through
270° about point C.

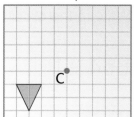

**d)** Rotate the shape through
180° about point D.

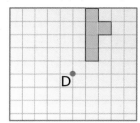

You need to
use a ruler to draw
the new shapes.
Count the squares
carefully.

Shape A is **rotated 180°** about the **point P**.

**Draw shape A** in its **new** position on the diagram below.

You may use tracing paper.

You may use an angle measurer.

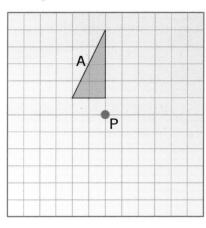

Answers and Guidance are given on pp.41–42.

*How long did you take?*

**21**

# National Test Questions 2

🕐 *You should be able to complete these questions in 10 minutes*

**1**  Write in the missing number.

$$864 \div \boxed{\phantom{xxx}} = 45$$

*1 mark*

**2**

Jack's wooden bricks measure 3 cm by 3 cm by 4 cm.

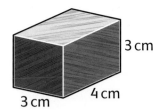

3 cm

4 cm

3 cm

Jack puts them into a tray like this.

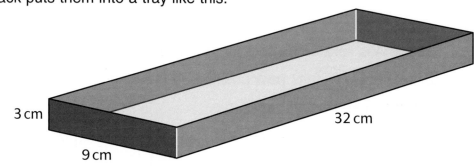

3 cm

32 cm

9 cm

Work out the largest number of bricks which can lie flat in the tray.

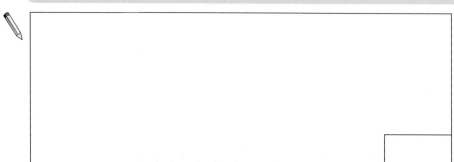

*1 mark*

**22**

# National Test Questions 2

**3** Write a **different** number in **each** of these boxes so that the **mean** of the **three** numbers is **9**.

☐ ☐ ☐

*1 mark*

Write a number in each of these boxes so that the **mode** of the **five** numbers is **11**.

☐ ☐ ☐ ☐ ☐

*1 mark*

**4** Look at the shape on the grid.

Turn it through **one right angle** around the point **A**.

Draw its new position.

You may use tracing paper.

*1 mark*

Answers and Guidance are given on pp.46-47. ***How long did you take?***

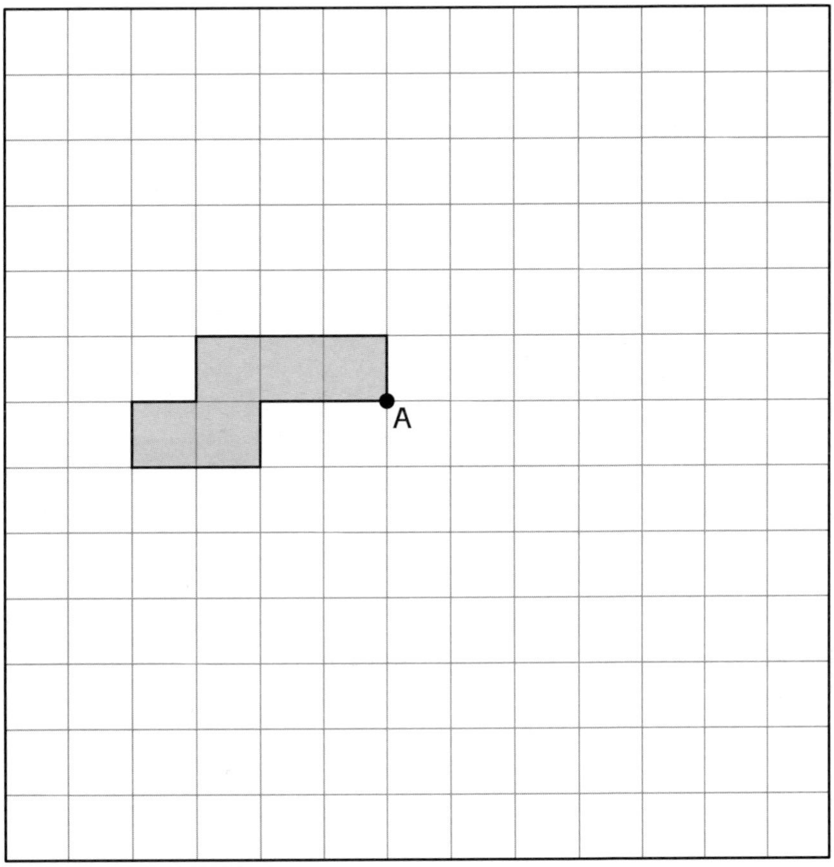

# 9 Time

**What's it all about?**

★ This chapter gives you practice in using the 12-hour clock and the 24-hour clock.

★ It checks that you understand how to read timetables.

★ It also reminds you how to calculate the time in different time zones.

A clock with hands is an **analogue** clock. The hands move round and can show any time.

A clock with just numbers is a **digital clock**. It 'jumps' from one minute (or second) to the next.

**1** Timetables, clocks and watches use either the 24-hour or the 12-hour clock. Write the time equivalents for each of these times. The first two have been done for you.

a) 13.30 = 1.30 p.m.

b) 8 a.m. = 08.00

c) 14.15

d) 12.20

e) 11.59 p.m.

f) 11.59 a.m.

g) 12.14 a.m.

h) 12.14 p.m.

i) 18.14

j) 22.08

k) 18.47

l) 3 p.m.

**2** Use this bus timetable to answer the questions.

| | Departure times | | | | |
|---|---|---|---|---|---|
| **Liskeard** | 06.14 | 08.17 | 12.32 | 17.46 | 23.05 |
| **Upton Cross** | 06.31 | 08.35 | 12.48 | 18.04 | 23.22 |
| **Coads Green** | 07.06 | 09.14 | 13.22 | 18.41 | 23.57 |
| **Launceston Castle** | 07.19 | 09.28 | 13.36 | 18.58 | 00.10 |
| **Launceston town centre** | 07.21 | 09.30 | 13.38 | 19.00 | 00.12 |
| **London** | | | | | |

a.m. stands for **ante-meridiem** or after twelve o'clock midnight but before twelve o'clock midday.

p.m. stands for **post-meridiem** or after 12 o'clock midday but before 12 o'clock midnight.

a) I want to go from Liskeard to Launceston town centre. Which is the fastest bus? How long does it take?

b) If I go on the first bus in the morning, how long does it take to go from Upton Cross to Launceston Castle?

c) If I take the last bus at night, how long does it take to go from Upton Cross to Launceston Castle then?

d) Which bus takes the longest time to travel from Liskeard to Coads Green?

e) A coach leaves Launceston for London five minutes after each bus arrives at Launceston town centre. It takes 6 hours and 20 minutes to reach London. Complete the timetable by adding the London arrival times.

Midday is written 12 noon or 12.00. Midnight is 12 midnight or 00.00. Do not use either a.m. or p.m. when it is exactly 12 o'clock midday or midnight.

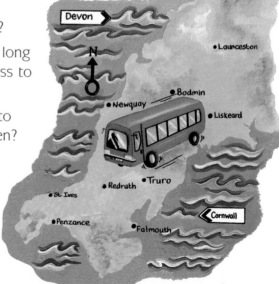

**3** Solve these problems about time.

**a)** Here is a page from a calendar.

| April | | | | | | |
|-------|-----|-----|-------|-----|-----|-----|
| Mon | Tues | Wed | Thurs | Fri | Sat | Sun |
| | | | | 1 | 2 | 3 |
| 4 | 5 | 6 | 7 | 8 | 9 | 10 |
| 11 | 12 | 13 | 14 | 15 | 16 | 17 |
| 18 | 19 | 20 | 21 | 22 | 23 | 24 |
| 25 | 26 | 27 | 28 | 29 | 30 | |

   i) Jack's birthday is on 5th April. Tara's is four weeks and five days later. What is the date of her birthday?
   ii) How many Sundays will there be in May of the same year?

**b)** Lucy leaves home at ten past eight in the morning. She arrives home at twenty-five to five.
   i) How long has she been away from home?
   ii) Write the time she arrives home, using the 24-hour clock.

**c)** Time zones

The time in Boston, USA, is 5 hours behind the UK.
The time in Los Angeles, USA, is 8 hours behind the UK.
The time in Sydney, Australia, is 10 hours ahead of the UK.
The time in Athens Greece, is 2 hours ahead of the UK.

Complete this table.

GMT stands for Greenwich Mean Time. In the summer in the UK we put the clock forward one hour and the time then is called **British Summer Time (BST)**.

Calculate the UK time first.
This makes deciding whether to add or subtract easier.

| UK time (GMT) | Boston time | Los Angeles time | Sydney time | Athens time |
|---------------|-------------|------------------|-------------|-------------|
| 06.00 | | | | |
| | quarter past 7 in the evening | | | |
| 19.00 | | | | |
| | | | 14.17 | |
| | | 9.45 p.m. | | |
| 11.43 a.m. | | | | |
| | | | | 21.30 |

## Test question

Here is Lucy's timetable.

| | 9.00 | | 10.30 10.45 | | 12.00 13.00 | | 14.00 | | 15.30 |
|--|------|--|-------------|--|-------------|--|-------|--|-------|
| Monday | English | | Maths | | PE | | History | | |
| Tuesday | Maths | | English | | Science | | Art | | |
| Wednesday | English | | Maths | | Geography | | RE | | |
| Thursday | Maths | | English | | Music | | Design and Technology | | |
| Friday | English | | Maths | | Science | | Games | | |

How long is she in school each day?

How much more time does she have studying English than history?

Answers and Guidance are given on pp.42–43.

*How long did you take?*

# 10 Interpreting data

**1** This diagram shows the distance of different towns from Central London.

> Notice the towns are in bands. The bands are 0–8 miles, 8–16 miles, 14–24 miles, over 24 miles.

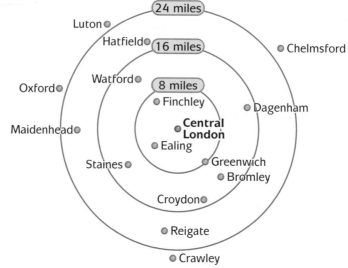

**a)** Write down the name of a town which is between 8 and 16 miles from central London.

**b)** Write the names of two towns that are more than 24 miles from London.

**c)** How many towns on the diagram are between 16 and 24 miles from central London?

**d)** How far from central London is Ealing?

**2** This diagram shows the distances in kilometres between six towns.

|  | Dover | Glasgow | Liverpool | Norwich | Plymouth | York |
|---|---|---|---|---|---|---|
| **Dover** |  | 799 | 486 | 277 | 459 | 448 |
| **Glasgow** | 799 |  | 355 | 606 | 789 | 341 |
| **Liverpool** | 486 | 355 |  | 384 | 477 | 163 |
| **Norwich** | 277 | 606 | 384 |  | 565 | 290 |
| **Plymouth** | 459 | 789 | 477 | 565 |  | 544 |
| **York** | 448 | 341 | 163 | 290 | 544 |  |

> To read this chart, find the first town in the row along the top, and the second town in the column down the left-hand side. Read across from the second town until you meet the column headed by the first town. The square where they meet shows the distance between the two.

**a)** How far is it from:
  **i)** Liverpool to York      **ii)** Norwich to Glasgow      **iii)** Dover to York?

**b)** If I travel from Dover to Norwich and then on to Plymouth, how many kilometres have I travelled?

**c)** The petrol tank in my car only holds enough petrol for me to travel 300 km. Between which towns can I travel without stopping for petrol?

**Conversion graphs or diagrams are used to convert between different measurement units, such as miles and kilometres, pounds (£) and dollars ($), degrees centigrade or Celsius (°C) and degrees Fahrenheit (°F).**

**3 a)** Estimate the reading in Fahrenheit degrees (°F) if the temperature is 12°C.

**b)** Estimate the reading in Fahrenheit degrees if the temperature is −10°C.

**c)** Estimate the reading in Celsius degrees (°C) if the temperature is 64°F.

**d)** Estimate the reading in Celsius degrees if the temperature is 72°F.

**e)** Estimate the reading in Fahrenheit degrees if the temperature is 35°C.

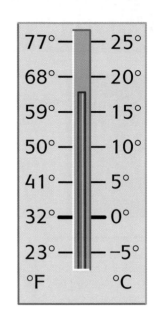

**In questions 3(e) and 4(e) you will need to do more than simply read the charts. Think carefully!**

**4 a)** How many dollars will I get for £2.50?

**b)** How many dollars will I get for £3.25?

**c)** How many pounds will I get for $2.00?

**d)** How many dollars will I get for £3.00?

**e)** If I have $50.00, how much do I have in pounds?

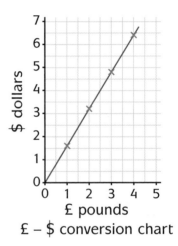

£ – $ conversion chart

---

**Test question**

At a petrol station there is a scale for converting litres and gallons.

Approximately how many **litres** are there in **3 gallons**?

Give your answer to the **nearest litre**.

☐ litres

Approximately how many **gallons** are there in **7 litres**?

Give your answer to **1 decimal place**.

☐ gallons

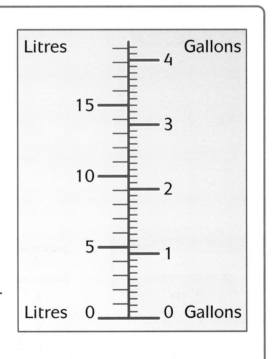

---

Answers and Guidance are given on pp.43-44.

 **How long did you take?** ☐

# 11 Angles

> When drawing angles you need to use an angle measurer or **protractor**.

**1** Draw these angles accurately.

a) 75°  c) 125°  e) 63°

b) 35°  d) 145°  f) 87°

**2** Rotate these clock hands clockwise through 90°. The first one has been done for you.

a)   b)   c)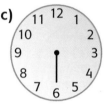

> Always draw in pencil – and make sure it is really sharp!

**3** Rotate these clock hands clockwise through 180°.

> 90° = ¼ turn
>
> 180° = ½ turn
>
> 270° = ¾ turn

a)   b)   c) clock showing hand pointing to 3

**4** Rotate these clock hands clockwise through 270°.

a)   b)   c)

Two pairs of parallel sides

parallelogram

two equal angles & two equal sides

isosceles triangle

Two pairs of parallel sides. All sides are equal in length

rhombus

four right angles & two pairs of equal sides

rectangle

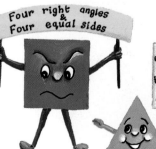

Four right angles & Four equal sides

square

three equal sides & three equal angles of 60°

equilateral triangle

**5** Look at these sketches, then draw the shapes at their correct sizes. Label each shape with its name. Measure and mark the sizes of all the angles inside each shape.

a)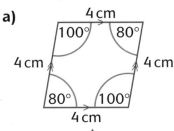

d)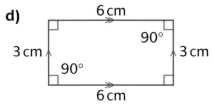

b)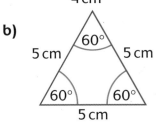

e)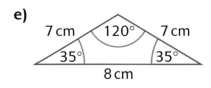

c)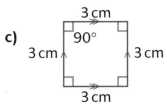

f)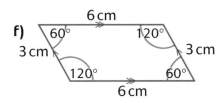

**6** Draw these shapes from the instructions given.

a)  A square with sides of 8 cm

b)  An equilateral triangle with sides of 6 cm

c)  A rectangle with sides of 3 cm and 7 cm

d)  An isosceles triangle with two angles of 45° and one side of 9 cm. Measure and mark the lengths of the other two sides.

## Test question

This is a design for an arrowhead.

Below is part of a larger scale drawing of the arrowhead.

The drawing has the same size angles as the design.

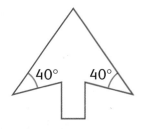

**Draw two more lines to complete the arrowhead accurately.**

Use an angle measurer (protractor).

You will need to trace or copy the lines onto a larger sheet of paper.

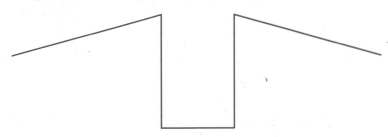

Answers and Guidance are given on p.44.

 **How long did you take?**

# 12 Solving problems

**What's it all about?**

★ This chapter gives you practice in solving problems where you have to think about changing units.

★ In your Maths National Test, you will be asked to solve problems using addition, subtraction, multiplication and division.

> When we change units, we are **converting** the number from one unit to another.

**1** When you solve problems you sometimes need to change the way a number is written before you do the calculation.

Change the units of these numbers. The first one is done for you.

a) £647.71 = 64 771 pence

b) 65 m = **?** mm

c) 57 pence = £ **?**

d) 91 litres = **?** ml

e) 7300 metres = **?** kilometres

f) 67.19 kg = **?** grams

**2** Fill in the correct units for these amounts.

a) £5.30= 530 **?**

b) 33.4 l = 3340 **?**

c) 1950 m = 1.95 **?**

d) 876 cl = 8.76 **?**

e) 2630p = **?** 26.30

f) 1473 mm = 1.473 **?**

g) 3460 ml = 3.46 **?**

h) 3.62 m = 3620 **?**

i) 28.49 kg = 28 490 **?**

j) 4.2 l = 4200 **?**

> Think whether the number has been multiplied or divided by 10, 100 or 1000.

**3** Solve these problems.

a) For each loaf a baker produces, he requires 840 g of flour. How much flour will he need if he bakes 225 loaves? Give your answer first in grams and then in kilograms.

b) There are 125 runners in a race. Each drinks 750 ml of water. What was the total quantity of water drunk? Give you answer first in millilitres and then in litres.

> Remember: Always show your working. In the Maths National Test you may get a mark even if you make a mistake in the calculation.

c) A man walks 1734 metres each day. How far does he walk in 14 days? Give your answer first in metres and then in kilometres.

d) Ice creams cost 75p each. An ice cream seller sells 382. How much money does she take altogether? Give your answer first in pence and then in pounds.

> You will find using a calculator helpful here.

e) *Neighbours* lasts 25 minutes. If I watch 28 episodes, how long have I spent watching the television? Give your answer first in minutes and then in hours.

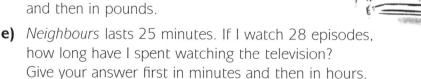

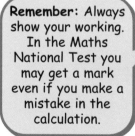

**4** When you solve problems, you have to make sure that the numbers you are using in your calculations are written in the same units. Solve the following problems. Write how you would need to convert the units and what method to use. The first one has been done for you.

You need to be really sure about conversion facts, for instance that there are 1000 ml in a litre.

Start by deciding what type of maths you need to use to solve problems like these.

Many of them are better done on a calculator. However, you need to know how to do the maths in case they occur when you haven't a calculator to hand!

**a)** Tickets for a car park cost 30p per car. The total money taken in a day is £285.00. How many cars used the car park?

**Conversion:** convert £285.00 to pence → 28 500 p
**Method:** 28 500 ÷ 30
**Answer:** 950 cars

**b)** A newspaper seller takes a total £37.40. If he sold each newspaper for 20p, how many papers did he sell?

**c)** A lemonade bottling plant used 1575 litres of lemonade. How many 25 centilitre bottles did they fill?

**d)** A ruler-making factory uses 2135 m of plastic strip every week. Each ruler requires 35 cm of plastic strip. How many rulers are produced in a week?

**e)** A cola-canning factory uses 2081 litres of cola every day. How many 330 ml cans are filled in a day?

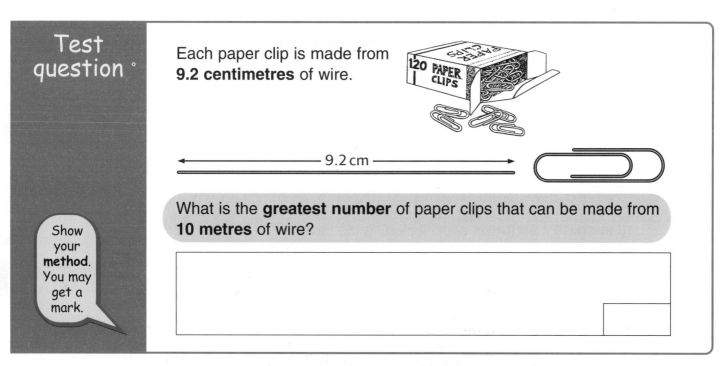

Test question °

Each paper clip is made from **9.2 centimetres** of wire.

←———————— 9.2 cm ————————→

What is the **greatest number** of paper clips that can be made from **10 metres** of wire?

Show your **method**. You may get a mark.

---

Answers and Guidance are given on pp.44-45.

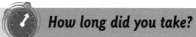 *How long did you take?*

⏱ *You should be able to complete these questions in 17 minutes*

**1**   Here is the calendar for August 1998.

| August 1998 | | | | | | |
|---|---|---|---|---|---|---|
| Sunday | Monday | Tuesday | Wednesday | Thursday | Friday | Saturday |
| | | | | | | 1 |
| 2 | 3 | 4 | 5 | 6 | 7 | 8 |
| 9 | 10 | 11 | 12 | 13 | 14 | 15 |
| 16 | 17 | 18 | 19 | (20) | 21 | 22 |
| (23) | 24 | 25 | 26 | 27 | 28 | 29 |
| 30 | 31 | 1 | 2 | 3 | 4 | 5 |

Simon's birthday is on **August 20th**.

In 1998 he had a party on the **Sunday after** his birthday.

What was the **date** of his party?

August 23rd.

*1 mark* ✓

Tina's birthday is on **September 9th**.

On what **day of the week** was her birthday in 1998?

Wednesday

*1 mark* ✓

**2**   Mrs Jones prints books.

| PRINT CHARGES |
|---|
| 3p per page |
| 75p for the cover |

Jon pays £4.35 for his book, including the cover.

*Show your **method**. You may get a mark.*

How many pages are in his book?

34·35  
− 0·75  
3·60

1·20  
3)3·60

3)360 ✓

120 ✓

*2 marks*

3   This diagram shows the distances of different towns from Birmingham.

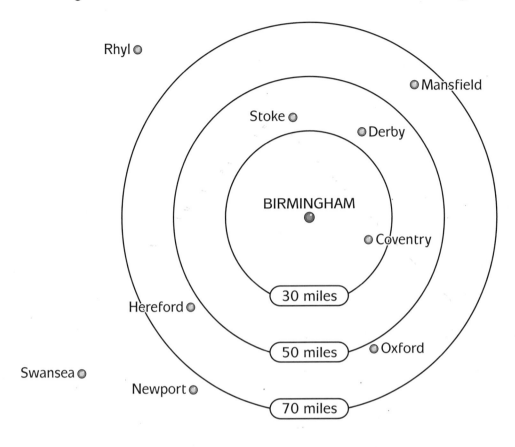

Write the name of a town which is **between 30 and 50 miles** from Birmingham.

STOKE

✓

1 mark

Use the diagram to estimate the distance in miles from **Birmingham** to **Mansfield**.

62 miles

✓

1 mark

**4**  Here is a sketch of a triangle.

It is not drawn to scale.

**Draw the full size triangle accurately, below.**

Use an angle measurer (protractor) and a ruler.

One line has been done for you.

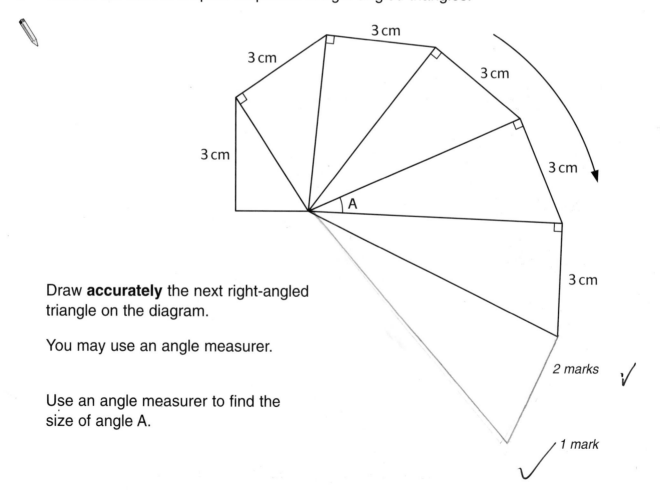

7 cm

48°

10 cm

*2 marks*

10 cm

✓ it
we had
prohactor )

**5**  Here is the start of a spiral sequence of right-angled triangles.

3 cm

3 cm

3 cm

3 cm

3 cm

3 cm

3 cm

A

Draw **accurately** the next right-angled
triangle on the diagram.

You may use an angle measurer.

*2 marks* ✓

Use an angle measurer to find the
size of angle A.

*1 mark* ✓

**6**   This table shows the distances in kilometres between five towns.

|  | Birmingham | Cardiff | London | Manchester | Newcastle |
|---|---|---|---|---|---|
| **Birmingham** |  | 179 | 188 | 127 | 334 |
| **Cardiff** | 179 |  | 269 | 278 | 489 |
| **London** | 188 | 269 |  | 298 | 441 |
| **Manchester** | 127 | 278 | 298 |  | 212 |
| **Newcastle** | 334 | 489 | 441 | 212 |  |

Use the table to find the distance from **London to Manchester**.

298 km

*1 mark*

James goes from **Newcastle** to **Birmingham**, and then on to **Cardiff**.

Show your method. You may get a mark.

How many **kilometres** does he travel?

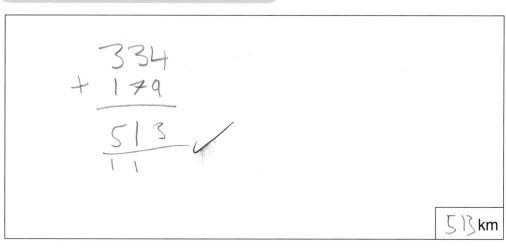

334
+ 179
─────
513
  1 1

513 km

*2 marks*

Answers and Guidance are given on pp.47–48.   *How long did you take?*

# Answers and Guidance

All of the Test questions in this book are at level 5.

## 1 Fractions of shapes

This chapter builds on work done in Book 2, Chapter 11 Equivalent fractions and Book 3, Chapter 6 Fractions, Chapter 11 Percentages and Chapter 12 Pie charts.

**1** b) $\frac{1}{3}$ is shaded     c) $\frac{1}{8}$ is shaded     d) $\frac{1}{8}$ is shaded

If any of your answers were wrong, did you divide up the whole shape with dotted lines as you were shown in the example? The diagrams should look like this.

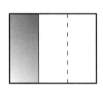 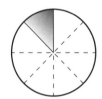 

If your answers were wrong for parts (c) and (d), did you realise that the fraction of a shape may be the same even though the shape is different?

**2** b) $\frac{2}{3}$ is shaded     c) $\frac{5}{6}$ is shaded     d) $\frac{5}{8}$ is shaded

If any of your answers were wrong, did you divide up the whole shape with dotted lines as you were shown in the example? The diagrams should look like this.

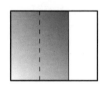  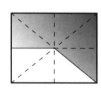

**3** From question 1:

a) $\frac{1}{4} \times 100 = $ **25%**     c) $\frac{1}{8} \times 100 = $ **12.5%**

b) $\frac{1}{3} \times 100 = $ **33.3%**     d) $\frac{1}{8} \times 100 = $ **12.5%**

From question 2:

a) $\frac{7}{12} \times 100 = $ **58.3%**     c) $\frac{5}{6} \times 100 = $ **83.3%**

b) $\frac{2}{3} \times 100 = $ **66.7%**     d) $\frac{5}{8} \times 100 = $ **62.5%**

If any of your answers were wrong, did you remember how to convert a fraction to a percentage?

**4** b) $\frac{3}{4} \times 400 = $ **300 kg**

c) $\frac{2}{3} \times 1000 = $ **667 kg** (to the nearest kg)

d) $\frac{1}{5} \times 500 = $ **100 kg**

If any of your answers were wrong, did you:
- divide up the shape as you did in questions 1 and 2
- estimate the fractions accurately
- complete the calculations correctly?

**5** **Shop C** sold the most bananas.

Your explanation should show that you calculated the weight of bananas sold by each shop and then compared them to find which sold the most. You might have said:

Shop A sold $\frac{1}{3}$ of 600 kg = 200 kg, Shop B sold $\frac{1}{4}$ of 900 kg = 225 kg and Shop C sold $\frac{3}{8}$ of 800 kg = 300 kg. So Shop C sold the most.

If any of your answers were wrong, did you:
- understand that you had to do a calculation in this case, and that looking at the size of the division on the pie charts may be misleading
- calculate each shop's sales correctly?

### Test question

Mrs Binns gets $\frac{1}{4} \times £1000 = $ **£250** from selling peaches.

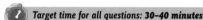 *Target time for all questions: 30–40 minutes*

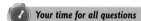 *Your time for all questions*

## 2 Using your calculator

This page builds upon the work done in Book 1, Chapter 12 Using calculators. It also builds on the maths in many other chapters of the books in this series.

**1** b) **770.4**     e) **1331.64**     i) **2620**
   c) **451.5**     g) **11.25**     j) **15.25**
   d) **86.32**     h) **99.44**

If any of your answers were wrong, try again. Be very careful that you key the numbers and symbols in correctly.

**2** b) **£12.05**
   c) **£19.50**
   d) **£9.1875** *or* **£9.19**
   e) **£513.20**

Remember that your answers to (c) and (e) are not correct if you have left the final zero off.

**3** b) **£5.34** *or* **534p**
   c) **£9.54** *or* **954p**
   d) **£6.50** *or* **650p**
   e) **£13.80** *or* **1380p**

If any of your answers were wrong, check that you either converted the pence into £s by writing them as a decimal, or converted the £ into pence by multiplying by 100.

# Answers and Guidance

**4** b) **0.5**
c) **0.75**
d) **0.2**
e) **0.4**
f) **0.125**
g) **0.33 (to 2 dp)**
h) **0.8**
i) **0.625**

$\frac{1}{8}, \frac{1}{5}, \frac{1}{3}, \frac{3}{8}, \frac{2}{5}, \frac{1}{2}, \frac{5}{8}, \frac{3}{4}, \frac{4}{5},$

*or* **0.125, 0.2, 0.33, 0.375, 0.4, 0.5, 0.625, 0.75, 0.8**

If any of your answers were wrong, did you:
● use the decimal equivalents to help answer the last part of the question
● take notice of the second decimal place figure as well as the first?

**5** There are lots of these, for instance, $\frac{1}{9} = 0.111\ 111$ (or 0.11 to 2 dp). You need to ask an adult to help you check your answers.

**6** b) **1500**   c) **306**   d) **2**   e) **5.5**

To work these out correctly you need to work slowly and carefully through the steps.

**7** a) **£3041.50**
b) **25.4**
c) **15.2**
d) **111** days
e) **9636** people

If any of your answers were wrong, did you:
● key in the numbers carefully
● read, copy and interpret the display properly
● have an answer close to your estimate?

## Test question

a) **£6331.90**
b) **943 programmes**

You should have keyed in the numbers like this:

a) ⟨2⟩⟨7⟩⟨5⟩⟨3⟩⟨×⟩⟨2⟩⟨.⟩⟨3⟩⟨=⟩

**Display shows: 6331.9**
**Answer: £6331.90 – you must write this final 0!**

b) ⟨6⟩⟨1⟩⟨2⟩⟨.⟩⟨9⟩⟨5⟩⟨÷⟩⟨.⟩⟨6⟩⟨5⟩⟨=⟩

**Display shows: 943**
**Answer: 943 programmes**

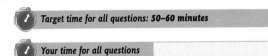
*i* Target time for all questions: **50–60 minutes**

*i* Your time for all questions

# 3 Area and perimeter

These pages build on work in Book 1, Chapter 8 Perimeters, Book 2, Chapter 5 Area and Book 3, Chapter 8 Area and perimeter.

**1** b) can split into

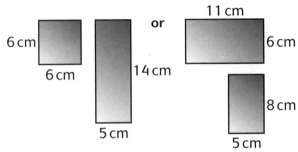

c) can split into

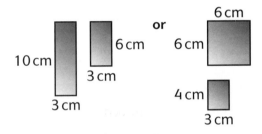

d) can split into

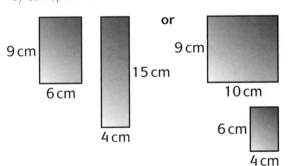

e) can split into

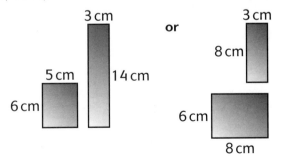

If any of your answers were wrong – especially the measurements – look again at the shapes and make sure that you understand how each measurement is worked out from the information given.

# Answers and Guidance

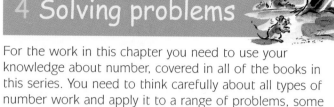

**2** b) **70** cm² and **36** cm² *or* **66** cm² and **40** cm²
  c) **30** cm² and **18** cm² *or* **36** cm² and **12** cm²
  d) **54** cm² and **60** cm² *or* **90** cm² and **24** cm²
  e) **30** cm² and **42** cm² *or* **24** cm² and **48** cm²

If any of your answers were wrong, did you:
● use the formula and multiply the base measurement by the height for each rectangle
● multiply correctly?

**3** b) **106** cm²
  c) **48** cm²
  d) **114** cm²
  e) **72** cm²

If any of your answers were wrong:
● check your addition
● ask an adult to draw you some more shapes which can be divided into two parts, and try again.

**4** b) **50** cm    c) **32** cm    d) **50** cm    e) **44** cm

If any of your answers were wrong, check:
● that you really understand how to calculate a perimeter – look back at Book 1, Chapter 8 Perimeters and Book 3, Chapter 8 Area and perimeter
● your addition.

## Test question

Area = **49** cm²

Perimeter = **34** cm

To calculate the area you needed to split the shape into two rectangles:

$3 \times 3 = 9$ and $4 \times 10 = 40$ then add to give
$9 + 40 = 49$ cm².

To calculate the perimeter you needed to add:

$3 + 3 + 3.5 + 4 + 10 + 4 + 3.5 + 3 = 34$ cm.

 *Target time for all questions: 25–35 minutes*

 Your time for all questions

## 4 Solving problems

For the work in this chapter you need to use your knowledge about number, covered in all of the books in this series. You need to think carefully about all types of number work and apply it to a range of problems, some simple and some more difficult.

**1** b) **45 + 46 + 47 = 138**
  c) **33 + 34 + 35 = 102**
  d) **74 + 75 + 76 = 225**

If any of your answers were wrong, did you remember to make a rough estimate by dividing by 3?

By the time you had done one or two examples, did you see that the answer is always:

$\frac{1}{3}$ of the answer less $1 + \frac{1}{3}$ of the answer $+ \frac{1}{3}$ of the answer plus 1?

**2** b) **84 × 6 = 504** *or* **72 × 7 = 504**
     *or* **63 × 8 = 504** *or* **56 × 9 = 504**
  c) **64 × 7 = 448** *or* **56 × 8 = 448**
  d) **96 × 8 = 768**
  e) **87 × 4 = 348** *or* **58 × 6 = 348**
  f) **77 × 7 = 539**

If any of your answers were wrong, did you:
● use what you know about number for example to see that the single digit could not be 5 in any of the examples
● divide the answers by the possibilities correctly?

**3** b) **18 × 18 = 324**
  c) **7 × 7 × 7 = 343**
  d) **13 × 13 × 13 = 2197**
  e) **12 × 12 × 12 = 1728**
  f) **17 × 17 × 17 = 4913**

Did you use your knowledge to deduce the rough size of the number correctly?

**4** There are several different solutions to each of these problems. Ask an adult to help you check. Make sure that you check that the carrying figures in the addition sums do not take you over the target numbers.

## Test question

**(23 × 23) − 23 = 506**

 *Target time for all questions: 60–70 minutes*

 Your time for all questions

# Answers and Guidance

## 5 Division

The work in this chapter builds on previous work in Book 2, Chapter 2 Division.

1  b) **700 ÷ 20 = 35**
   c) **400 ÷ 40 = 10**
   d) **600 ÷ 30 = 20**
   e) **900 ÷ 60 = 15**
   f) **600 ÷ 40 = 15**
   g) **1000 ÷ 20 = 50**
   h) **900 ÷ 10 = 90**

If any of your answers were wrong, did you:
- round the numbers correctly
- divide accurately?

2  a) **9.1**
   b) **31.22**
   c) **9.33**
   d) **18.29**
   e) **15.21**
   f) **13.57**
   g) **58.35**
   h) **63.71**

If any of your answers were wrong, did you:
- key in the numbers correctly
- look at the third figure after the decimal point when you wanted to round the numbers to 2 dp
- remember to round numbers under 5 down and numbers 5 or over up?

3  b) **23**

$$\begin{array}{r} 23 \\ 37\overline{)851} \\ \underline{74} \\ 111 \\ \underline{111} \\ 0 \end{array}$$

   c) **36**

$$\begin{array}{r} 36 \\ 14\overline{)504} \\ \underline{42} \\ 84 \\ \underline{84} \\ 0 \end{array}$$

   d) **32**

$$\begin{array}{r} 32 \\ 24\overline{)768} \\ \underline{72} \\ 48 \\ \underline{48} \\ 0 \end{array}$$

   e) **34**

$$\begin{array}{r} 34 \\ 27\overline{)918} \\ \underline{81} \\ 108 \\ \underline{108} \\ 0 \end{array}$$

   f) **54**

$$\begin{array}{r} 54 \\ 18\overline{)972} \\ \underline{90} \\ 72 \\ \underline{72} \\ 0 \end{array}$$

   g) **23**

$$\begin{array}{r} 23 \\ 41\overline{)943} \\ \underline{82} \\ 123 \\ \underline{123} \\ 0 \end{array}$$

   h) **22**

$$\begin{array}{r} 22 \\ 45\overline{)990} \\ \underline{90} \\ 90 \\ \underline{90} \\ 0 \end{array}$$

If any of your answers were wrong, we have given you the working, so go through it carefully and try to find where you have difficulty. You might need an adult to help you with this.

4  b) **27 r 11**

$$\begin{array}{r} 27 \quad r\,11 \\ 23\overline{)632} \\ \underline{46} \\ 172 \\ \underline{161} \\ 11 \end{array}$$

   c) **30 r 18**

$$\begin{array}{r} 30 \quad r\,18 \\ 21\overline{)648} \\ \underline{63} \\ 18 \end{array}$$

   d) **11 r 3**

$$\begin{array}{r} 11 \quad r\,3 \\ 35\overline{)388} \\ \underline{35} \\ 38 \\ \underline{35} \\ 3 \end{array}$$

   e) **32 r 3**

$$\begin{array}{r} 32 \quad r\,3 \\ 18\overline{)579} \\ \underline{54} \\ 39 \\ \underline{36} \\ 3 \end{array}$$

   f) **14 r 13**

$$\begin{array}{r} 14 \quad r\,13 \\ 34\overline{)489} \\ \underline{34} \\ 149 \\ \underline{136} \\ 13 \end{array}$$

# Answers and Guidance

g) **31 r 10**

$$24 \overline{)754}$$
$$\underline{72}$$
$$34$$
$$\underline{24}$$
$$10$$

**5** a) **29.55**
  b) **27.48**
  c) **30.86**
  d) **11.09**
  e) **32.17**
  f) **14.38**
  g) **31.42**

**6** a) $26\frac{4}{24}$ *or* $26\frac{1}{6}$
  b) $21\frac{19}{37}$
  c) $21\frac{1}{28}$
  d) $25\frac{12}{19}$
  e) $27\frac{8}{32}$ *or* $27\frac{1}{4}$
  f) $37\frac{3}{23}$

**7** a) **83.44**
  b) **83.39**
  c) **72.12**
  d) **35.14**
  e) **147.57**
  f) **14.93**

## Test question

$$16 \overline{)572} \quad \overset{35 \quad r\,12}{}$$
$$\underline{48}$$
$$92$$
$$\underline{80}$$
$$12$$

*or* $35\frac{12}{16}$ *or* $35\frac{3}{4}$ *or* **35.75**

 *Target time for all questions: 60–70 minutes*

 *Your time for all questions*

## 6 Volume

The work in this chapter builds on work about area in Book 2, Chapter 5 Area and Book 3, Chapter 8 Area and perimeter.

**1** b) **32** cm³   c) **16** cm³   d) **20** cm³   e) **20** cm³

You will find the correct answers if you count carefully!

**2** b) **80** cm³ **Working** 20 × 4 = 80
  c) **66** cm³   d) **40** cm³   e) **77** cm³

Again, you will find the correct answer by counting carefully.

**3** a) 3 × 3 × 3 = **27** cm³
  b) 6 × 5 × 3 = **90** cm³
  c) 5 × 4 × 4 = **80** cm³
  d) 3 × 4 × 2 = **24** cm³

If any of your answers were wrong, check your multiplication carefully.

**4** a) **2** cm

**Working:**   Volume = width × length × height
          16 cm³ = width × 4 cm × 2 cm
          width = 2 cm

b)

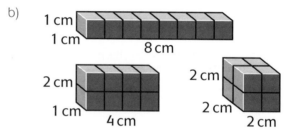

If you did not find all three answers, did you:
● remember *all* the factors of 8 (1, 2, 4, 8)
● use the factors to work out the possible lengths
● remember that a cube is also a cuboid?

## Test question

**24** cm³

Any of these combinations:

**2 cm, 3 cm, 5 cm**
**1 cm, 6 cm, 5 cm**
**1 cm, 3 cm, 10 cm**
**1 cm, 1 cm, 30 cm**

It does not matter which lengths you made the width, length and height, as long as all your numbers were within one combination.

 *Target time for all questions: 20–30 minutes*

 *Your time for all questions*

# Answers and Guidance

## 7 Mean, mode and median

The work in this chapter is at level 5.

**1** b) **6**    c) **7**    d) **46**    e) **124**

If any of your answers were wrong, did you:
- add the groups of numbers carefully
- divide by the number of numbers accurately
- use (or check your answers with) a calculator?

**2** a) **38** runs: 304 ÷ 8 = 38
   b) **£68**
   c) **420** vouchers
   **Working:** If the mean was 14 and the number in the class 30, the total number of vouchers was 14 × 30 = 420.
   d) **16** mm
   **Working:** If the mean for the three days was 12 mm, the total rainfall must have been 12 × 3 = 36 mm.
   The rainfall for the first 2 days was 20 mm, so the rainfall on the last day was 36 – 20 = 16 mm.

**3** b) **23**
   c) **56**
   d) **11 and 13** (This group is bi-modal, both 11 and 13 appear five times.)

**4** a) **12**    b) **2**    c) **30p**
   d) You need to have written five different sets of numbers. In **each set** the number 17 must occur the greatest number of times. One example is **13, 14, 17, 17, 17, 12**. Ask an adult to check for you.

**5** b) 20, 21, 28, 35, 40, 41, 42; **35** is the median score
   c) £59, £60, £64, £74, £83; **£64** is the median wage
   d) 25p, 25p, 30p, 30p, 30p, 35p, 40p, 40p, 40p, 45p, 50p; **35p** is the median

**6** a) mean: **28**, mode: **26**, median: **27**
   b) mean: **35p**, mode: **30p**, median: **35p**
   c) mean: **£33**, mode: **£38**, median: **£35**
   d) mean: **10.9**, mode: **10.7** and **11.2** both occur twice, median: **10.8**

If any of your answers were wrong, make quite sure you understand that:
- the mean requires you to add all the numbers together and then divide by the number of numbers
- the mode is the most commonly occurring score
- the median requires you to put the numbers in order of size and then find the middle score.

### Test question

Christine's mean jump is **3.5** m, the mode is **3.4** m and the median is **3.4** m

 **Target time for all questions: 40–50 minutes**

 **Your time for all questions**

## 8 Rotational symmetry

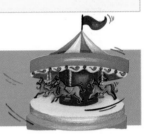

The work in this chapter builds on previous work in Book 1, Chapter 11 Reflective symmetry and Book 3, Chapter 10 Reflective symmetry.

**1** b)

c)

d)

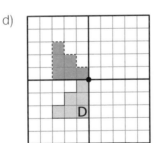

# Answers and Guidance

**2** a)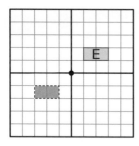
c)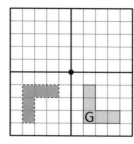

b)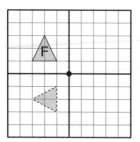
d)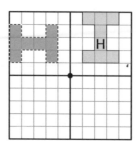

If any of your answers to questions 1 and 2 were wrong, did you:
- rotate the shape through the correct angle (number of degrees)
- trace the shape and rotate it
- keep the shape the correct distance from the point about which you were rotating?

**3** b)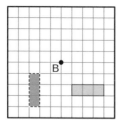
d)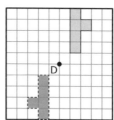

c)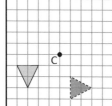

If any of your answers were wrong, did you:
- use tracing paper and a protractor to rotate the shape the correct amount
- make sure that the shape was rotated about the correct point?

If you are still unsure, look back through the chapter and then try again.

## Test question

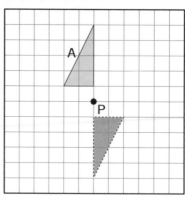

If your answer was wrong, did you:
- follow the same method as for question 3, above
- make sure you rotated the shape clockwise
- keep all points in the image the same distance from point P?

Look back through the chapter, if you still need more practice.

 **Target time for all questions: 30–40 minutes**

 **Your time for all questions**

# 9 Time

This chapter builds on work in Book 1, Chapter 2 Using timetables.

**1** c) **14.15 = 2.15 p.m.**    h) **12.14 p.m. = 12.14**
   d) **12.20 = 12.20 p.m.**    i) **18.14 = 6.14 p.m.**
   e) **11.59 p.m. = 23.59**    j) **22.08 = 10.08 p.m.**
   f) **11.59 a.m. = 11.59**    k) **18.47 = 6.47 p.m.**
   g) **12.14 a.m. = 00.14**    l) **3 p.m. = 15.00**

**2** a) The 12.32 bus takes **1 hour and 6 minutes.** The others take 1.07, 1.13, 1.14 and 1.07 respectively.
   b) **48** minutes
     **Working:** 07.19 – 06.31 = 48 minutes
   c) **50** minutes
     **Working:** 00.12 – 23.22 = 50 minutes
   d) The 08.17 bus takes **57** minutes
   e) The last row in the timetable should look like this:

| London | 13.46 | 15.55 | 20.03 | 01.25 | 06.37 |
|---|---|---|---|---|---|

To get these answers right you need to work very carefully.

Did you remember the additional 5 minutes waiting time in Launceston?

**3** a) i) **8th May**  ii) **5 Sundays**
b) i) **8 hours 25 minutes**  ii) **16.35**
c)

| UK time (GMT) | Boston time | Los Angeles time | Sydney time | Athens time |
|---|---|---|---|---|
| 06.00 | 01.00 | 22.00 | 16.00 | 08.00 |
| quarter past midnight | quarter past 7 in the evening | quarter past 4 in the afternoon | quarter past 10 in the morning | quarter past 2 in the morning |
| 19.00 | 14.00 | 11.00 | 05.00 | 21.00 |
| 04.17 | 23.17 | 20.17 | 14.17 | 06.17 |
| 5.45 a.m. | 12.45 a.m. | 9.45 p.m. | 3.45 p.m. | 7.45 a.m. |
| 11.43 a.m. | 6.43 a.m. | 3.43 a.m. | 9.43 p.m. | 1.43 p.m. |
| 19.30 | 14.30 | 11.30 | 05.30 | 21.30 |

You might have written some of these times in a different way – for instance using the 24-hour clock instead of the 12-hour clock. If you have done this, you will need help to check your answers.

If any of your answers were wrong, make sure you remembered whether a time difference was ahead or behind the given times, and that you did the arithmetic correctly.

Did you notice the hint always to start by calculating the UK time?

## Test question

Each school day is **6 hours and 30 minutes** long.

Lucy studies English as follows:

| | |
|---|---|
| Monday | 1 hour and 30 minutes |
| Tuesday | 1 hour and 15 minutes |
| Wednesday | 1 hour and 30 minutes |
| Thursday | 1 hour and 15 minutes |
| Friday | 1 hour and 30 minutes |
| **Total:** | 7 hours |

She studies history for 1 hour and 30 minutes on Mondays.

The difference is **5 hours and 30 minutes**.

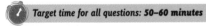
*Target time for all questions: 50–60 minutes*

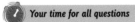
*Your time for all questions*

## 10 Interpreting data

This unit builds on work in Book 1, Chapter 9 Using bar graphs, Book 2, Chapter 9 Line graphs and Book 3, Chapter 12 Pie charts.

**1** a) Any one of **Staines, Watford, Croydon, Bromley or Dagenham**
b) Any two of **Oxford, Chelmsford, Luton or Crawley**
c) **3: Hatfield, Maidenhead and Reigate**
d) **Between 5 and 7 miles**

If any of your answers were wrong, did you:
● look carefully at each circle
● identify correctly the towns within each circle
● make a reasonable estimate of the distance between Ealing and London?

**2** a) i) **163 km**  ii) **606 km**  iii) **448 km**
b) **842 km**
Total journey Dover to Norwich 277 km plus Norwich to Plymouth 565 km
c) **Dover to Norwich** *or* **Norwich to Dover**, **Liverpool to York** *or* **York to Liverpool**, **Norwich to York** *or* **York to Norwich**

If any of your answers were wrong, try again. Perhaps a ruler would help you follow the rows and columns more accurately.

**3** a) **53°F** *or* **54°F**  d) **22°C** *or* **23°C**
b) **14°F**  e) **95°F**
c) **17°C** *or* **18°C**

Did you read the chart carefully and extend it where necessary? If you had difficulty with parts (b) and (e), did you *either* try drawing an extension of the chart *or* work out that 5°C = 9°F and use this information to calculate the answer?

**4** a) **$4.00**  d) **$4.80**
b) **$5.00–$5.20**  e) **£30.00–£35**
c) **£1.20–£1.30**

If you had difficulty reading the line graph, look back at Book 2, Chapter 9.

# Answers and Guidance

In part (e) you needed to have found a simple conversion from the graph and then multiplied this to complete the conversion, for instance, you could have found how much you would get for $1.00 (60p) and multiplied by 50, £0.60 × 50 = £30.00.

## Test question

a) **14** litres (between 13.5 and 13.7 litres, which is 14 litres to the nearest litre)

b) **Between 1.5 and 1.6** gallons, so an answer of 1.5 or 1.6 gallons is acceptable, to 1 dp.

*Target time for all questions: 25–35 minutes*

*Your time for all questions*

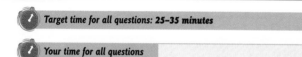

# 11 Angles

The work in this chapter builds on previous work in Book 1, Chapter 3 Drawing 2D shapes, Book 2, Chapter 1 Properties of shape and Book 2, Chapter 10 More properties of shape.

In all the questions in this chapter your drawings **must** be accurate.

In the National Test you must be within 2 mm or 2° to gain a mark.

**1** Check your angles with your protractor. If you have difficulty, ask an adult to recheck them for you.

**2** b)  c)

**3** a)  b)  c)

**4** a)  b)  c)

If any of your answers to questions 2, 3 and 4 were wrong:

● if you have done this by measuring the angles, check your measurement – you might need to practise this skill more with other angles

● if you realised that you could count round the clock face, check you counted 3 numbers for question 2, 6 numbers for question 3 and 9 numbers for question 4.

**5** a) **rhombus**
b) **equilateral triangle**
c) **square**
d) **rectangle**
e) **isosceles triangle**
f) **parallelogram**

**6** Ask an adult to check the accuracy of your drawings.

## Test question

When you check your drawing, check that the two angles are **both** between 38° and 42°. The angle formed at the top of the arrow will be between 96° and 104°.

Ask an adult to check your measurements.

*Target time for all questions: 55–65 minutes*

*Your time for all questions*

# 12 Solving problems

The work in this chapter builds upon that in Book 1, Chapter 10 Solving problems, Book 3, Chapter 1 Multiplication and division by 10, 100, 1000 and Book 3, Chapter 9 Conversion of units.

**1** b) **65 000** mm
c) **£0.57**
d) **91 000** ml
e) **7.3** km
f) **67 190** g

If any of your answers were wrong, make sure you know all the conversions. Look back to Book 3, Chapter 9 Conversion of units.

**2** a) **pence**
b) **centilitres**
c) **kilometres**

# Answers and Guidance

d) **litres**
e) **pounds**
f) **metres**
g) **litres**
h) **millimetres**
i) **grams**
j) **millilitres**

If any of your answers were wrong, did you check whether:
● the number had been multiplied by 10, 100 or 1000
● you used the correct conversion?

**3** a) **189 000 grams, 189 kilograms**
b) **93 750 millilitres, 93.75 litres**
c) **24 276 metres, 24.276 kilometres**
d) **28 650 pence, £286.50**
e) **700 minutes, 11 hours 40 minutes**
   or **11.67 hours**

If any of your answers were wrong, did you:
● multiply the numbers correctly, either using long multiplication or a calculator – refer to Book 3, Chapter 1 Multiplication and division by 10, 100, 1000, Book 3, Chapter 3 Multiplying larger numbers and Book 4, Chapter 2 Using your calculator
● divide your answer by the correct number to convert it to the required unit of measurement?

**4** b) **Conversion:** £37.40 to pence or 20p to pounds
**Method:** 3740 ÷ 20 or 37.4 ÷ 0.2
**Answer: 187** newspapers

c) **Conversion:** 1575 litres to centilitres
            or 25 cl to litres
**Method:** 157 500 ÷ 25 or 1575 ÷ 0.25
**Answer: 6300** bottles

d) **Conversion:** 2135 m to centimetres
            or 35 cm to metres
**Method:** 213 500 ÷ 35 or 2135 ÷ 0.35
**Answer: 6100** rulers

e) **Conversion:** 2081 litres to millilitres
            or 330 ml to litres
**Method:** 2 081 000 ÷ 330 or 2081 ÷ 0.33
**Answer: 6306** cans – there is a remainder but this is not sufficient to make a whole can. Refer to Book 2, Chapter 12 Solving problems for rounding answers.

If any of your answers were wrong, did you:
● convert the units correctly
● divide by the correct amount
● do this division correctly either by using a calculator (see Chapter 2 Using your calculator), or by long division (see Chapter 5 Division)?

## Test question

**108** paper clips

If you got this wrong, did you:
● *either* convert the 10 metres of wire to centimetres correctly by multiplying by 100 and divide your converted number by 9.2
   *or* convert 9.2 cm to metres by dividing by 100 and then divide 10 by 0.092
● remember you needed to count only complete paper clips?

 *Target time for all questions: 35–45 minutes*

 *Your time for all questions*

# Answers and Guidance

**1** The pointer is most likely to stop on **3**.

Your answer needs to say something like:
'More space is taken up by the number 3 than any other number' *or* 'There is a $\frac{4}{12}$ ($\frac{1}{3}$) chance of spinning a 3 which is more than any other number' *or* 'The number 3 takes up four sections on the inner ring. This is more than any other number.'

The probability of spinning an even number is $\frac{4}{12} = \frac{1}{3}$.

(There are two sections with the number 4, two sections with the number 2. There are no other even numbers.)

| CROSS-CHECK | **CHAPTER 1** Fractions of shapes |

**2** a) **£1.50**

If your answer was wrong, did you:
- multiply the correct number of flowerpots (3)
- use the correct value for the flowerpots (£12.95 each)
- add on to this total the cost of one spade (£9.65)
- find a total of £48.50
- subtract this from £50.00 (leaving £1.50)?

b) **6**

If your answer was wrong, did you:
- divide £10 by £1.45 correctly (remembering to divide 10.00 by 1.45 or 1000 by 145)
- round your answer down because you are looking for whole packets of seeds?

| CROSS-CHECK | **CHAPTER 2** Using your calculator |

**3** The perimeter of the shape is **80 cm**.

If your answer was wrong, did you:
- see that the triangles overlapped one another
- see that you needed to subtract the base measurement of 5 cm from 12 cm (7 cm)
- see that there were four triangles used
- calculate 4 × 13 cm = 52 cm and 4 × 7 cm = 28 cm
- then calculate 52 cm + 28 cm = 80 cm?

| CROSS-CHECK | **CHAPTER 3** Area and perimeter |

**4** The answer is **53 × 7 = 371**.

If your answer was wrong, did you:
- notice that the answer to the question (371) ended in a 1
- recall that only the 3, 7 and 9 times tables have answers ending in a 1
- see that the question wanted whole numbers
- try dividing 371 by 3 (123.6666)
- try dividing 371 by 9 (41.2222)
- try dividing 371 by 7 (53)?

| CROSS-CHECK | **CHAPTER 4** Solving problems |

**1** 864 ÷ 19.2 = **45**

If your answer was wrong, did you:
- use a calculator for this question
- divide 864 by 45?

| CROSS-CHECK | **CHAPTER 5** Division |

**2** **24** bricks

If your answer was wrong, did you either:
- work out the volume of each brick as 3 × 3 × 4 = 36 cm²
- work out the volume of the tray as 3 × 9 × 32 = 864 cm²
- divide 864 cm by 36 cm to get 24?

*or*:
- notice that each brick was the same height as the tray and therefore the bricks would be one deep
- see that the tray would fit three bricks across its width (9 ÷ 3 = 3)
- notice that the length of the tray (32 cm) was the length of eight bricks
- see that the largest number of bricks would therefore be:
  1 deep
  3 across
  8 long
  and if these numbers are multiplied together 8 × 3 × 1 = 24?

| CROSS-CHECK | **CHAPTER 6** Volume |

# Answers and Guidance

**3** **8, 9, 10** *or* **7, 9, 11**, *or* **1, 8, 18** *or...*

You could have written any three numbers that have a total of 27, to give a mean of 9.

**1, 2, 11, 11, 15** *or* **5, 11, 13, 11, 19**, *or* **11, 12, 11, 13, 11** *or...*

You could have written any set of numbers in which there were more elevens than any other number. Five elevens would also be correct.

**CROSS-CHECK** **CHAPTER 7** Mean, mode and median

**4** Your finished drawing should look like this.

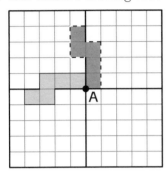

You would also get a mark for this, although it is usual to turn a shape clockwise unless you are told otherwise.

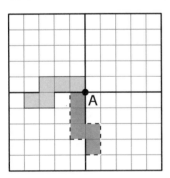

If your answer was wrong, did you:
- use tracing paper
- rotate the shape, not reflect it
- move it through 90° around point A?

**CROSS-CHECK** **CHAPTER 8** Rotational symmetry

---

## National Test Questions 3

**1** a) **23rd August, 1998**
b) **Wednesday**

If either of your answers was wrong, did you:
- count on from 20th August to the next Sunday
- count on from the end of August for nine days?

**CROSS-CHECK** **CHAPTER 9** Time

**2** **120** if one cover is used or **95** if two covers are used.

If your answer was wrong, did you:
*either*
- subtract 75p from £4.35 (£4.35 – 75p = £3.60)
- divide £3.60 by 3p to find out the number of pages (3.60 ÷ 0.03 or 360 ÷ 3 = 120)

*or*
- subtract £1.50 (2 covers @ 75p) from £4.35 (£4.35 – £1.50 = £2.85)
- divide £2.85 by 3p to find the number of pages (2.85 ÷ 0.03 or 285 ÷ 3 = 95)?

**CROSS-CHECK** **CHAPTER 12** Solving problems

**3** a) **Stoke** *or* **Derby**
b) **60–65** miles

If either of your answers was wrong, did you:
- identify which towns are in the 30–50 mile circle
- notice that only Stoke and Derby are in that circle
- see that Mansfield is just over midway in the 50–70 mile circle
- estimate the distance as between 60 and 65 miles?

**CROSS-CHECK** **CHAPTER 10** Interpreting data

**4** Ask an adult to check your drawing for you. If your drawing was not accurate, did you:
- begin by drawing an accurate base line of 10 cm
- measure an angle of 48° on the right side of the baseline
- check your work, to make sure it was accurate?

**CROSS-CHECK** **CHAPTER 11** Angles

# Answers and Guidance

**5** Angle A = **65°**.

Ask an adult to check your drawing. It should look like this.

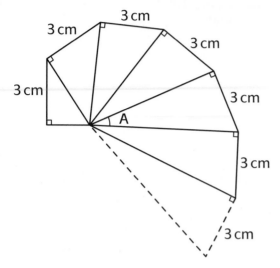

If your answer was wrong, did you:
- line up you angle measurer correctly
- draw a line of length 3 cm
- make sure you drew the line at an angle of 90°
- measure the angle A correctly by placing the angle measurer in the correct place?

**CROSS-CHECK**   **CHAPTER 11** Angles

**6** a) **298** kilometres
   b) **513** kilometres

If either of your answers was wrong, did you:
- find London on the chart
- read across to find Manchester
- note that where they met the total was 298 kilometres

*then*
- read the distance from Newcastle to Birmingham (334)
- add to that the distance of Birmingham to Cardiff (179) to find the total (513 km)?

**CROSS-CHECK**   **CHAPTER 10** Interpreting data